LIFE balance

Robert Warren //
Sue Mayfield

LIFE balance

a 5-session course //
on rest, work and play //
for Lent //

CHURCH HOUSE
PUBLISHING

Church House Publishing
Church House
Great Smith Street
London SW1P 3NZ

Tel: 020 7898 1451
Fax: 020 7898 1449

ISBN 0 7151 4079 5

Published 2005 by
Church House Publishing

Copyright © Sue Mayfield
and Robert Warren 2005

Cover design by Andy Stonehouse

Printed by Creative Print and
Design Group, Ebbw Vale, Wales

Contents

Acknowledgements

The authors and publisher gratefully acknowledge permission to reproduce copyright material in this book. Every effort has been made to trace and contact copyright holders. If there are any inadvertent omissions we apologize to those concerned and will ensure that a suitable acknowledgement is made in all future editions.

Special thanks are due to Gordon Mursell, Bishop of Stafford, for kindly allowing the authors to use unpublished material from his research notes.

Extracts from the New Revised Standard version of the Bible, Anglicized Edition (NRSV): copyright © 1989, 1995 by the Division of Christian Education of the National Council of Churches of Christ in the United States of America, and used by permission. All rights reserved.

Extracts from the Contemporary English Version of the Bible (CEV): copyright © American Bible Society 1991, 1995.

Extract from *God of Surprises* by Gerard Hughes, copyright © 1985. Used by permission of Darton, Longman & Todd.

>> Introduction

Life Balance is an opportunity to examine our patterns of rest, work and play, and to look afresh at our values and life principles in the light of the Bible's teaching about the Sabbath.

>>What is Sabbath?

A large pot had been in the possession of a family for more time than they could remember. It had served a number of purposes during that time and was currently being used as an umbrella stand in the hall. When a TV Road Show was in the area doing valuations, one of the children persuaded the parents – just for a bit of fun – to take the pot along. It proved to be a very rare vase, worth a small fortune.

The Sabbath is rather like that. We all have it, it has been around for ages, we have put it to all sorts of uses, but most of us have only the haziest idea what it was meant for. And we do not realize what a treasure it is!

> > **Sabbath is a gift** more than a demand. It is the gift of a break from the routines of life and a means of refreshing us. For Jews, celebrating Sabbath from sunset to sunset, Sabbath begins with the gifts of food and sleep. For Christians, celebrating Sabbath on the *first* day of the week, Sabbath is not so much the gift of rest at the end of a hard week's work, as a reminder (at the start of a new week) that the whole of life is sustained by God's grace and generosity.

> > **Sabbath is a door** opening up a new dimension – taking us beyond the necessary, the urgent and the everyday. Sabbath is not so much a day for *not* doing things (despite misconceptions reinforced by both Pharisees and Victorians!) but rather a day for *doing* the really important things: giving and receiving rather than buying and selling; enjoying the goodness and reality of God's presence and the beauty of his world. Sabbath is about entering into the fullness of life Christ promised here on earth as a foretaste of the richness of heavenly life.

> **Sabbath is an attitude** not just a day. Sabbath invites us to take its principles of resting, thanksgiving, justice and generosity into the whole of life – reducing the stress and rush and enlarging our vision.

> **Sabbath is a surprise!** The story of Creation in the opening verses of Genesis has a fascinating twist at the end. For seven days God creates spaces, habitats and living creatures. On the last day God rests, and makes holy, Sabbath time. This has striking relevance for us in a society that has been described as 'cash rich, time poor'. We talk of 'finding time', 'spending time', 'catching up', 'chasing our tails'. What we do not talk about is receiving time as gift or valuing it as holy.

>>Why study Sabbath during Lent?

Lent and Sabbath (be it Sabbath days or longer 'Sabbatical' periods) are seasons of stopping. Both are opportunities to pause, to find new rhythms, to create space and to clear some of the clutter in our overcrowded and lopsided lives.

Both Lent and Sabbath are about:

> **Time:** taking 'time out', making special 'holy' time to refocus mind and spirit and refresh the whole of life.

> **Spiritual disciplines:** Sabbath is one of the most neglected spiritual disciplines. We may practise prayer, fasting, giving and service but forget to practise Sabbath – even though it is one of the Ten Commandments.

> **Good news:** understanding Sabbath is a wonderful antidote to our frantic and fragmented culture. Sabbath can be an oasis in the desert of activity and a pole star in the dark night of the soul.

> **Sharing:** Though solitude is an important part of Lent and Sabbath, our experience of both is enhanced by community. We are called not just to share Sabbath but also to *give* Sabbath to others.

It is our hope and prayer that *Life Balance* will help us – as we work, rest and play – to:

> > discover the beauty of Sabbath principles in our daily lives;
> > build Sabbath time into the crazy pressures of shift patterns, complicated family structures and our 24/7 consumer culture;
> > find patterns for living that liberate rather than legislate.

In an age that has lost its soul, Sabbath keeping offers the possibility of gaining it back. In an age desperately searching for meaning, Sabbath keeping offers a new hope . . . The delight of the Sabbath and its resting, embracing and feasting give new energy and meaning to life as its climax and focal point.

Marva J. Dawn, Keeping the Sabbath Wholly, *p. 50*

>>What does the course consist of?

The course consists of **five sessions** for group study, each designed to last about **90 minutes**.

> > **Session 1** looks at the concept of Sabbath as a whole and invites group members to consider their own rhythms of work, rest and play.
> > **Sessions 2–5** take an in-depth look at Sabbath principles of celebration, rest, play and liberation.
> > **Session 5** also allows time for summary and reflection on the whole course. If you have time, you might want to do this as an extra session rather than doing this as part of session 5.

Each session contains study guidelines, interactive activities and ideas for prayer and meditation. (See pages 7–10 for a fuller description of the features of each session.) There are also ideas for practical action and suggestions for further study.

>>Who is the course for?

The course is designed for group study and many of the activities involve sharing together. An ideal size for the group would be between 8 and 12 people.

If your group is larger than 8, you might like to divide it into two smaller groups for the *Talk about it* sections of the sessions, allowing each small group to focus in more depth on just a few of the discussion questions and then feed back their responses to the whole group.

To get the most from the course, we suggest that each group member has a copy of the book.

>>Where should we meet?

The best meeting place for a course of this kind is probably someone's home. Alternatively, you could meet in a church hall or other community venue. Wherever you meet, make sure the venue is welcoming, comfortable, warm and easy for everyone to get to. If you are splitting into two groups it is good, where possible, to have these groups in separate rooms, as two groups in the same room tend to distract each other. However, if this isn't an option make sure that each 'huddle' sits close enough to each other to hear, without disturbing the other group(s) in the room.

You may like to provide refreshments before or after the course, in which case be aware that you will need to add on extra time to the recommended 90-minute session.

>>Who can lead the course?

This material has been designed so that most people, with a little preparation and thought, could lead it. You do not need to be a theological expert or experienced in adult education (although experience does, of course, help).

The leader's main task is not to teach or lecture the group, but to enable discussion and exploration by group members by leading them through the material provided.

As well as preparing and handling the study material and ensuring that prayer and meditation times go well, the leader should be aware of the dynamics of the group and alive to the joys and struggles of each group member. You might also make the coffee!

Leading a group study can be a big task if attempted by one person on his or her own, so you might like to consider sharing the leadership with someone else.

Remember that growth in the Christian life is not just about accumulating knowledge. There are things to learn here, but, more importantly, group members will be encouraged to reflect upon and to share their own experiences of life and of their learning during the course.

To help you in the task of group leadership, we offer the following 'tips'. You may find the booklet *Leading an Emmaus Group* helpful.

>>Tips for leaders

Be prepared

Make sure that you are familiar with the content of each session. You will need to decide beforehand which parts of the material you are going to use and whether you are going to split into smaller groups for some of the activities.

For each session we have provided background information to help with understanding concepts and the Bible passages. Make sure you read this information thoroughly. It is there to help you. It is not designed to be used verbatim in the session: this could very easily kill discussion. The aim of each session is to help group members towards a discovery of the meaning of Sabbath for themselves rather than telling them what to think. Additional background information is available on the web site (www.chpublishing/lifebalance) should you want to go a stage deeper, or feel you need more background information.

If you are responsible for the 'Input' part of the *Encounter* section, prepare what you will say in advance. Try not to say too much or to waffle. Make a few points clearly and well. You might like to practise what you will say so that when it comes to it you won't need to have your nose in your notes!

Delegate

Don't do everything yourself. Share out tasks with co-leaders or other group members. Not only does this help the leader, but it also gives others the chance to exercise and develop their own gifts of leading and contributing to the group.

You might ask someone to read one of the Bible passages or to lead an opening prayer or the closing meditation. You might delegate the role of welcoming people or making the refreshments. You could invite someone else to be a group 'enabler', if you decide to split into smaller groups.

Make sure you give people plenty of warning and don't land them with difficult tasks at the last minute. Be there to offer support and advice if needed. If you designate someone as a group enabler, give that person the opportunity to look at the material beforehand.

Be organized

> Try to arrive at the venue in good time so that you are not doing last minute preparations as people are arriving.

> Set up the room carefully, arranging the furniture so that there is a good group dynamic, with no one left out and everybody able to see the leader (and flipchart or video if you are using one).

> Make sure that you have pens, pencils, large sheets of paper, and any craft materials, music or objects ready beforehand. There is a checklist of everything you might need, at the beginning of each session.

Be imaginative

We know that people learn in different ways: some people like to take in information by reading and reflection in quiet, others learn best through group discussion, others like to respond to visual stimuli (e.g. a piece of art or a centrepiece used as a focal point in worship). Others like to respond through art and craft or through music.

The course provides you with a range of teaching methods and ideas. Suggestions are made – especially in the *Go deep* . . . sections – for creative, multimedia responses to Sabbath principles. We encourage you to be inventive and to draw on your own and the group's creativity, as appropriate.

Be flexible

We have provided enough material for a session of about 90 minutes but the suggested timings are only rough guides. You may find that you have too much material and need to miss out some of the activities. Feel free to do this. The parts of each session that are optional and could be cut without losing too much are marked with a *. Generally it is better to do a few activities thoroughly and well than to try to rush through everything and leave people exhausted.

Allow extra time for refreshments before or afterwards if you wish.

>>How each session works

Material for the course is in two sections for each of the five sessions – *Beforehand* and *The Session.*

Beforehand contains:

> **Aims** of the session – to help focus your mind in preparation and evaluate sessions after the event.

> **What you will need** – a checklist of practical materials required to ensure smooth running of the session. (See pages 11–13 for a more comprehensive list of resources.)

> **Background** to the Bible material – to help you understand Sabbath and its principles. Some groups might like to read this material for themselves either during the sessions or in advance. Alternatively it can be read by the leader or leaders and then summarized in the 'Input' section. *Background* material for Session 1 gives a general overview of Sabbath as an introduction to the whole course. *Background* material for Sessions 2–5 focuses on *Three key words* and a summary – *Cutting across* – of the ways in which Sabbath principles

challenge our values and lifestyle. This section also includes quotations from a variety of sources to stimulate further thought. Remember that there is more material on the web site if you want to use it (www.chpublishing/lifebalance).

The Session is structured under the following headings:

 Welcome

 Action replay

 Brainstorm

 Do something

 Encounter

 Talk about it

 Get real!

 Go deep . . .

Each session follows the same structure, though the *Do something* section comes before *Encounter* in Sessions 1 and 3 and after *Talk about it* in sessions 2, 4 and 5. The sections of the course work in the following ways (please note that timings are only approximate suggestions):

>>Welcome (5–10 minutes)

The leader welcomes the group and puts people at their ease. This is particularly important in the first session, especially if yours is a new group meeting for the first time. The notes for Session 1 give some suggestions of how to help a new group to gel.

Someone leads the group in prayer and/or the group says the Course Prayer together.

The purpose of this opening prayer is to still people from the busy-ness of the day and the rush of getting to the meeting, and to turn their thoughts to God. Each group will have its own preferences for how it prays. If the group is well established, it may already have a pattern for prayer. Suggestions are given in the session notes but feel free to use whatever is most appropriate for your group.

Remember: If you ask another member of the group to lead this part of the session, make sure there is plenty of time for preparation and guidance if needed. Ensure that no one does it under duress or feels 'dropped in it'.

>>Action replay [10 minutes]

An opportunity for group members to report on what they noticed, thought about, or did in response to the previous session's *Get real!* section.

>>Brainstorm [5 minutes]

A quick ice-breaker to be done individually, in pairs or as a whole group.

>>Do something [5–10 minutes]

A hands-on activity for the group to do together.

>>Encounter [15 minutes]

The group encounters themes of Sabbath via:

> **Input:** short talk from the leader based on his/her reading of the *Background* information. (This may be cut or omitted altogether if group members prefer to read the *Background* for themselves.)

> **Reading the Bible passages**.

>>Talk about it (25–30 minutes)

This is the main group study activity, consisting of questions for discussion, linking the Bible passages with Sabbath themes of pausing, celebration, rest, play and liberation. (Depending on numbers, you may wish to do this as a whole group or to split into two smaller groups and then report back to each other.)

An optional 'Jesus focus' links themes with incidents from Jesus' life.

>>Get real! (10 minutes)

Each week suggestions will be made for practical ways in which the group can put into practice the insights and values that have been discussed during the session. Projects may be individual tasks or whole group activities.

>>Go deep . . . (15 minutes)

This section offers an extended meditation to close the session. A number of suggestions are given to enable you to choose something appropriate to your group. Make sure this part is not omitted or rushed. This is a vital time to help the group to:

> slow down and reflect in silence on what has been the dominant theme for them and on what they feel has spoken to them through the session;

> grasp the meaning of Sabbath at a deep personal level;

> identify its application to their lives and to the wider community.

>>Resources

Music

We have suggested that you use music to prepare for prayer and during the *Go deep . . .* sections. The following recommendations might be useful:

> **Taizé** Several CDs available, including *Wait for the Lord* (Gia, 1995);

> **Instrumental Praise** Series of CDs (Brentwood, 1999);

> **Arvo Pärt**, *Litany* (ECM, 1996) or *Tabula Rasa* (HMV Classics, EMI, 1997);

> **Adiemus**, *Songs of Sanctuary* (Venture, 2001);

> **Smooth Classics** (Classic FM, 2002);

> **Music from the Late Late Service** – especially the CD *Deep Peace* (available from www.stickymusic.co.uk).

A number of other specific pieces of music are suggested at other points in the course:

Session 2

> 'What a Wonderful World', Louis Armstrong (*Louis Armstrong's All Time Greatest Hits* (MCA, 1994).

Session 3

> For the *Do something* activity, choose a relaxing piece of music from an album like *Smooth Classics* (see above).

> 'He's got the whole world in his hands', Nina Simone from *Nina: The Essential Nina Simone* (Metro, 2000).

Session 4

> For *Go deep . . .* use some upbeat jazz from an album such as *Classic Jazz: Jazz Masters* (Time Life Records, 2002) or some salsa music – try *Oxfam Salsa* (World Music Network, 2000).

Session 5

> 'Finale' and 'Gloria' from the *African Sanctus* by David Fanshawe (Silva Classics – SILKD 6003).

> 'The Touching Place', *Common Ground*, St Andrew Press, 1998.

> 'Travelling the road to freedom' from *A Touching Place*, Iona Community 1986.

> 'The Freedom Samba', *God in the Flesh*, Sticky Music, 1994.

Objects

You might like to place objects on a low table or on the floor as a visual focus during the *Welcome* or *Go deep* . . . sections. Suitable objects might be:

> flowers or a plant

> pebbles or stones

> candles

> twigs or driftwood

> a cross or crucifix

> a Bible

> a carving or figure, for example, of people praying or embracing.

Alternatively, you might like to arrange a collection of objects that reflect the theme of each session, changing each week. The following are suggestions of themed objects you could use:

> Session 1 – clocks, calendars, diaries, work tools;

> Session 2 – objects from the natural world, such as flowers, leaves, shells, fruit;

> Session 3 – pillows, bread, water, slippers, lavender;

> Session 4 – board games, sports equipment, musical instrument, paints, gardening things;

> Session 5 – ropes, chains, barbed wire, cross, images of freedom, e.g. birds in flight, butterflies, people leaping, skateboarders.

Ask group members to bring in objects that relate to the session's theme or share out responsibility for assembling the focus between group members.

Playdough recipe

Mix together to a smooth paste 2 cups plain flour, 2 cups water, 1 cup salt, 2 tablespoons cooking oil, 2 teaspoons cream of tartar, plus food colouring/flavouring. Place mixture in a saucepan and cook gently and very slowly over a low heat, stirring all the time, until the mixture forms a ball. The playdough should keep for a few weeks in an airtight container.

Images

If you want to use images of Christ as a visual focus try:

> *The Christ We Share* picture resource collection from CMS/USPG. (One of the cards featured in this pack is 'The Laughing Christ', which would be particularly appropriate for Session 4.)

> **Icon postcards** – many cathedrals, churches or religious bookshops sell postcard images. Alternatively, try using www.google.co.uk. Click on 'Images' and then type in 'religious icons'.

If you want images of rest, play, liberation or birds in flight try typing any of these words into www.google.co.uk – 'Images' – in the same way.

>> 1 Time to Pause/ Beforehand

>>Aim

This session aims to introduce the concept of Sabbath and to examine our rhythms of work, rest and play in the light of Sabbath principles.

What you will need (make your own selection)

> candles;

> music to encourage stillness (see page 11 for suggestions);

> objects to provide a visual focus (see page 12);

> flipchart or large sheet of paper and marker pens;

> A4 paper and pens;

> songbooks.

>>Background

Leaders: please see pages 7–8 for tips on how to use this material.

What is Sabbath?

> **Stillness** – The word 'Sabbath' comes from the Hebrew word *Shabbat*, which means to pause, to cease and to be still. Sabbath is the opportunity to get off the treadmill and reflect on our values and priorities.

> **Rhythm** – The pattern of resting one day in seven imitates the rhythm of creation in Genesis 1 where God worked creatively for six days and then paused to rest and to enjoy all that had been made.

> **Receiving** – Sabbath is a gift from God, a work of grace and a reminder that all we have comes from God's creative love. We do not so much 'practise' Sabbath as receive it.

> **Refreshment** – Sabbath is more than the cessation of work, it is about restoration, creativity and play – things that busy adults all too easily neglect.

> **Freedom** – Sabbath is about liberation, wholeness and well-being.

> **Holy** – God himself observes the Sabbath, modelling it for us. He calls it holy and exhorts us to do the same.

Sabbath is 'the climax of living . . .', 'a *palace in time* which we build . . .', and 'an opportunity to mend our tattered lives.'

Heschel, The Sabbath: Its Meaning for Modern Man, *pp. 14, 18*

How do you make a day holy? By seeing that it is holy already; and behaving accordingly.

Joy Davidman, Smoke on the Mountain, *p. 56*

Sabbath keeping is often disparaged as not useful, but we certainly do serve the world better out of the wholeness, order, revived spirits, empowered emotions, healthy bodies, renewed minds, authentic relationships, and nurtured sense of ourselves that Sabbath keeping creates.

Marva J. Dawn, Keeping the Sabbath Wholly, *p. 146*

Sabbath in the Old Testament

> Sabbath is about sharing in God's enjoyment of creation. Doing no work means going back from the curses of Genesis 3 to the generosity of Chapter 1. Sabbath is a return to Eden.

> The Ten Commandments give high priority to the Sabbath – it is to be kept, holy and treasured (Exodus 20.8-11).

> Sabbath is essential to the well-being of society – it is both communal (Deuteronomy 5.12-15) and environmental (Leviticus 25.1-12). Principles of justice and jubilee stem from the one in seven pattern that Sabbath establishes, which benefits all – foreigners, slaves and livestock included.

> Sabbath keeping is a reminder that all things come from God – that he is the source of life and salvation, that life is a gift.

When Israel wandered in the wilderness, even the provision of manna (Exodus 16.21-30) followed a Sabbath rhythm.

> Throughout history, Sabbath keeping has been a symbol of identity for the Jewish people (for example, during the Babylonian exile described in the Book of Daniel). In the Jewish tradition, Sabbath is a time for community events and shared feasts – celebrations of Holy Day (now secularized into 'holiday').

Jesus and the Sabbath

> As a Jew, Jesus observed the Sabbath.

> However, he challenged the Pharisees' hollow, hair-splitting observance of the rules of the Sabbath (Matthew 12.1-13; Luke 13.10-17), restoring the person-centredness and well-being that are at the heart of true Sabbath keeping (Isaiah 58.13,14). In Christ's time there were 1,521 things that you were banned from doing on the Sabbath – including rescuing a drowning man!

> Jesus saw Sabbath as being for the benefit of humankind, not vice versa (Mark 2.27) and as an opportunity to bless and enrich others (Matthew 12.12).

Sabbath in the Early Church

> In the Early Church, Christians celebrated Sunday (the first day of the Jewish week) as the 'Lord's Day' – the day of resurrection. This became (as Sabbath had for the Jews) a symbol of their Christian distinctiveness. The fact that it was the first day of the week and not the last emphasized grace over law – rest was given not earned – and the awareness that *all* of life was energized by God's love and goodness.

> Some Jewish Christians probably continued to observe the Sabbath (on Saturday) as well until 321 CE, when Constantine formally declared Sunday a day of rest.

> For the Early Church the Sabbath had extra meaning – it was a foretaste of the heavenly rest and a symbol of the age to come. Bede writes of '. . . the endless sabbath day of paradise where we shall live for ever with the saints'.

Sabbath in the twenty-first century

In our frantic, fragmented, pluralist society the pattern of a Sabbath rest one day in seven has been eroded and in many cases completely lost. But our overbusy, materialistic, technological culture needs to rediscover the rhythms of work, rest and play more than ever.

For many of us, our pattern of Sabbath keeping will, of necessity, need to be flexible.

It might include:

> **Sabbath days:** devoting a whole day (ideally one day a week but not necessarily always Sunday) to Sabbath activities of resting, enjoying, receiving, sharing, celebrating.

> **Sabbath moments:** taking the opportunity to be still, to receive, to appreciate, simply to enjoy. This can be done throughout the day in 'idle' moments such as waiting at traffic lights or while doing routine tasks.

> **Sabbath attitudes:** practising Sabbath moments helps us to develop attitudes of thanksgiving to God, appreciation of others and enjoyment of life, love and everything around us – right now. We 'press' Sabbath into the midst of our everyday lives.

> **Sabbath seasons:** extended resting/stopping/waiting periods, such as holidays, enforced (or chosen) redundancy, sabbaticals and career breaks challenge us to enjoy what *is* – for a season – and not to get frustrated by what *is not*. Responding creatively to such a 'season' is a way of practising Sabbath.

However we do it, practising and exploring Sabbath will have a profound effect on our well-being, our spirituality and our approach to life.

Cutting across

. . . a time-pressured, workaholic culture;

. . . materialism and acquisitiveness;

. . . the idea that non-productive time is time wasted;

. . . independence and self-sufficiency – being 'god' in our own lives;

. . . a tendency to undervalue relationships and family;

. . . cynicism and loss of wonder;

. . . the need to make ourselves feel important by seeming to be busy.

Come, let us welcome the Sabbath in joy and peace! Like a bride, radiant and joyous, comes the Sabbath. It brings blessings to our hearts; workday thoughts and cares are put aside. The brightness of the Sabbath light shines forth to tell that the divine spirit of love abides within our home. In that light all our blessings are enriched, all our griefs and trials are softened.

Prayer from the 'Kiddush' ritual for Sabbath eve

For detailed background notes on the Bible passages, go to www.chpublishing/lifebalance

>>Welcome (10 minutes)

Introduction

Make sure members of the group know each other's names
and are made to feel welcome. If this is a new group meeting for the
first time, invite members of the group to introduce themselves. You
could divide everyone into pairs, give the pairs five minutes to introduce
themselves to each other, then ask individuals to introduce their partner
to the rest of the group.

Pray

Create a still atmosphere. You might like to light a candle, play some
music or encourage people to focus on something that symbolizes
Sabbath stillness (see pages 11–12 for suggestions). Alternatively,
provide a visual resource such as a cross or image of Christ (see ideas
on page 13).

Either pray in your own words, asking God to help you as you begin your
course of study, or use the Course Prayer below. One person could read
it out or you could say it corporately.

Course Prayer

God of eternity, teach us to pause.
God of creation, teach us to wonder.
God of Sabbath, teach us to rest.
God of delight, teach us to play.
God of the poor, teach us to share in your work of liberation.
God of love, reconciling us through Christ Jesus,
fill our lives with your perfect peace. Amen.

>>*Brainstorm (5 minutes)

Ask the group: *What word, image or idea comes to mind when
you hear the word 'Sabbath'?*

Do this in whatever way suits the temperament of your group. Here are some suggestions:

> Ask people to shout out answers and write them on a flipchart or large sheet of paper.

> Ask people to compile lists in twos or threes and then read them out.

> Ask people to write one idea on a piece of paper and put it in a basket, then give the scraps of paper out again so everyone reads out someone else's contribution.

Try to give spontaneous answers and don't challenge or mock each other's suggestions.

>>Do something (15 minutes)

Give group members a sheet of paper each and invite them to draw a circle on it to represent an average week in their lives. Now ask them to calculate roughly what proportion of their time is spent in sleeping, eating, working, playing, relaxing, domestic maintenance, prayer and worship and other activities and to divide up their circle in 'pie chart' fashion. Encourage people not to worry unduly about scrupulous accuracy (no calculators, rulers or protractors!) but to see this as an approximate, at-a-glance representation of how they spend their time.

>>Encounter (20 minutes)

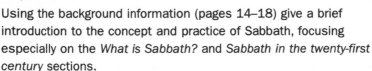

Input

Using the background information (pages 14–18) give a brief introduction to the concept and practice of Sabbath, focusing especially on the *What is Sabbath?* and *Sabbath in the twenty-first century* sections.

Alternatively, your group might prefer to read some or all of the pages for themselves.

Read
Exodus 20.8-11 (NRSV)

[8]Remember the sabbath day, and keep it holy. [9]For six days you shall labour and do all your work. [10]But the seventh day is a sabbath to the Lord your God; you shall not do any work – you, your son or your daughter, your male or female slave, your livestock, or the alien resident in your towns. [11]For in six days the Lord made heaven and earth, the sea, and all that is in them, but rested the seventh day; therefore the Lord blessed the sabbath day and consecrated it.

Mark 2.23 – 3.5 (NRSV)

[23]One sabbath he was going through the cornfields; and as they made their way, his disciples began to pluck heads of grain. [24]The Pharisees said to him, 'Look, why are they doing what is not lawful on the sabbath?' [25]And he said to them, 'Have you never read what David did when he and his companions were hungry and in need of food? [26]He entered the house of God, when Abiathar was high priest, and ate the bread of the Presence, which is not lawful for any but the priests to eat, and he gave some to his companions.' [27]Then he said to them, 'The sabbath was made for humankind, and not humankind for the sabbath; so the Son of Man is lord even of the sabbath.'

[1]Again he entered the synagogue, and a man was there who had a withered hand. [2]They watched him to see whether he would cure him on the sabbath, so that they might accuse him. [3]And he said to the man who had the withered hand, 'Come forward.' [4]Then he said to them, 'Is it lawful to do good or to do harm on the sabbath, to save life or to kill?' But they were silent. [5]He looked around at them with anger; he was grieved at their hardness of heart and said to the man 'Stretch out your hand.' He stretched it out, and his hand was restored.

>>Talk about it (25 minutes)

Consider some of or all the following questions:

> Exodus 20.8-11 commands people to cease from work one day in seven. Why do you think this is important? How is it practical in modern society?

> What is Jesus' approach to the Sabbath in Mark 2.23 – 3.5?

> What do you think Jesus meant when he said 'The Sabbath was made for humankind, and not humankind for the Sabbath' (v. 27)?

> What attitudes and values (e.g. stopping, enjoying, playing) do you associate with Sabbath? *Make a list together and keep it for future sessions.*

> Look at your pie chart. In the light of the two Bible passages, what is your response to your own rhythms and patterns?

> Why is Sabbath considered 'holy'? What does that teach you about your priorities?

*Jesus focus

Look at Jesus in Mark 1.32-38. This glimpse of Jesus' ministry shows him

> engaging with the clamour of people's needs;

> withdrawing for recuperative rest;

> making decisive choices in a replenished state.

What about Jesus' practice do you want to imitate?

>>Get real! (5 minutes)

Part of the aim of the course is to help group members to live out Sabbath principles in practical ways. The following are suggestions of things the group might like to do in the time before the next session.

> Think about your own patterns of work, rest and play during the following week. You might want to rethink the way you spend Sunday or your day/time off.

> If you are using the course during Lent, you might like to choose a Lenten discipline in which you:

>> give up or cut down on something that currently takes up a lot of your time;

>> take up something that you feel your life currently lacks such as a new 'play' activity.

> Start keeping a 'Sabbath notebook' in which you notice moments and situations where you experience 'Sabbath attitudes'. You can do this in written form or as a mental checklist. The next session will begin with an opportunity to share these observations.

>>Go deep . . . (10 minutes)

Create a still atmosphere. You could light a candle or play some music.

Choose some of the following activities as appropriate to your group:

> Sing 'Take my life and let it be' (*Mission Praise: Combined*, 624)

> Light some candles and say this prayer that Jewish families say at the start of the Sabbath as they light the 'Kiddush' candles:

Blessed art thou, O Lord our God, King of the universe.
May the Sabbath-light which illumines our dwelling cause peace and happiness to shine in our home.
Bless us, O God, on this holy Sabbath and cause divine glory to shine upon us.
Enlighten our darkness and guide us and all humanity, thy children, towards truth and eternal light. Amen.

Quoted by Marva J. Dawn in Keeping the Sabbath Wholly, *p. xvii*

Pray

Use one or more of the following prayers or pray in your own words.

When we are rushing and harassed
Be still and know that I am God.
When we are burdened and weary
Be still and know that I am God.
When we are bemused and perplexed
Be still and know that I am God.
When we feel sore or overlooked
Be still and know that I am God.
When we are smug and self-important
Be still and know that I am God.
When we think that we ourselves are God
Be still and know that I am God.

Timeless God,
help us to be still.
Creator God,
help us respond to your world.
God of comfort,
help us rest in you.
Playful God,
help us take ourselves less seriously.
Holy God,
suffuse us with the fragrance of Sabbath.
Amen.

Sabbath God,
help us to stop,
slow down,
unclench our fists
and receive.
Amen.

>> 2 Time to Celebrate/Beforehand

>>Aim

This session aims to celebrate our life in God and the delights of the created world and to focus our minds on habits of thankfulness, freedom from anxiety and the gift of the present moment.

What you will need (make your own selection)

> *candles;

> *music (see page 11 for suggestions);

> *objects to provide a visual focus for Sabbath celebration (see page 12);

> A4 paper and pens;

> *songbooks;

> *something to eat during *Do something*;

> video or DVD of *Chariots of Fire* (see page 69);

> *collage materials.

>>Background

Leaders: please see pages 7–8 for tips on how to use this material.

Three key words

Delight, Beauty, Gift

1 Delight

> In the account of creation in Genesis 1.1 – 2.3 the phrase 'God looked . . . and it was good' occurs seven times. The seventh time it is '*very* good'. God is pleased with all that he has made and on the seventh day he pauses in order to engage with it and savour it.

> We rest on the Sabbath because God has first done the same. In observing a Sabbath rhythm we share in God's sense of celebration, taking time to pause in thankfulness and delight. Philippians 4.4-6 emphasizes this principle of thankfulness.

Celebration is the honouring of that which we hold most dear. Celebration is delighting in that which tells us who we are. Celebration is taking the time to cherish each other. Celebration is returning with open arms and thankful hearts to our Maker.

Sara Wenger Shenk, Why Not Celebrate!, *pp. 2–3*

Celebration is about 'making all the right connections' with God, life, others, all creation – and ourselves. It is about the divine capacity to enjoy God, life and others.

Robert Warren, Being Human, Being Church, *pp. 120–121*

2 Beauty

> In the Jewish tradition there is an emphasis on beauty during the Sabbath. Special food is eaten and tables are laid with candles and 'best' tableware. There is an emphasis too on quality family time and rabbinic guidelines even include the injunction to married people to enjoy good sex on the Sabbath.

> Holocaust memorial collections of objects and items from daily life reveal that even in the concentration camps many Jews managed to make garments and Sabbath utensils with which to celebrate their holy time. In fact, celebration becomes all the more poignant and essential in times of struggle and hardship.

In difficult times you should always carry something beautiful in your mind.

Blaise Pascal, quoted in John O'Donohue,
Divine Beauty – the Invisible Embrace, *p. 27*

3 Gift

> Taking time to pause and celebrate forces us to live in the present moment. We recognize that this moment – like the whole of our lives and our salvation through Christ – comes as a gift from God.

> Freed from time pressures and from anxiety about past and future, we are able to get in touch with eternity and with the values of the kingdom. We dwell in the present moment, celebrating God's love, his tenderness and his saving work through Christ.

It is the grace of God in the whole of life to which Genesis points us. The riches of creation touch us most fully when we receive them with thanksgiving. Full humanity is experienced when life is consciously received and enjoyed as a gift and, thereby, as a relationship with the generous Giver. Living eucharistically (with thanksgiving) as creatures before the Creator is how life is meant to be lived and is a powerful antidote to a competitive and consumerist mentality.

Robert Warren, Being Human, Being Church, *pp. 116–17*

When you take time to travel with reverence, a richer life unfolds before you.

John O'Donohue, Divine Beauty, the Invisible Embrace, *p. 38*

Sabbath attitudes of celebration and thankfulness help us to engage more fully both with our everyday lives and with others – to operate at a deeper and more satisfying level. They free us from the lies of the advertising industry that possessions will give us joy and that craving bigger, better, or newer things will bring fulfilment.

Cutting across

. . . a preoccupation with past or future;

. . . a tendency to miss the moment – to have experiences but to miss the significance and holiness of them;

. . . cynicism and jaded appetites;

. . . self-pity and a negative 'Why me?' way of responding to hardships and difficulties.

This life is more than just a read thru' . . .

The Red Hot Chilli Peppers, 'Can't Stop'

>>Welcome (10 minutes)

Introduction

Welcome people back to the group and explain that this session considers the theme of Sabbath celebration.

Pray

Create an atmosphere of reverent celebration. You might like to:

> light candles;

> play some music (such as 'What a Wonderful World' by Louis Armstrong – see page 11 for details);

> encourage people to focus on something that symbolizes Sabbath celebration (see page 12 for suggestions). Alternatively, provide a visual resource such as a cross or image of Christ (see ideas on page 13).

Either pray in your own words, asking God to help you as you meet together, or use the Course Prayer. One person could read it out or you could say it corporately.

Course Prayer

God of eternity, teach us to pause.
God of creation, teach us to wonder.
God of Sabbath, teach us to rest.
God of delight, teach us to play.
God of the poor, teach us to share in your work of liberation.
God of love, reconciling us through Christ Jesus,
fill our lives with your perfect peace. Amen.

>>*Action replay (10 minutes)

Invite group members to talk about the things they did during the week as a result of the *Get Real!* part of the first session. Allow time for people to share snippets from their Sabbath notebooks if they have kept them. (Try to keep this focused and to avoid people going on at too great a length or turning this into a general 'news' time.)

>>*Brainstorm (5 minutes)

Share with other group members your most recent or most memorable experience of a celebration.

>>Encounter (15 minutes)

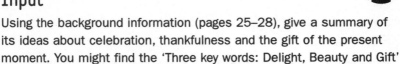

Input

Using the background information (pages 25–28), give a summary of its ideas about celebration, thankfulness and the gift of the present moment. You might find the 'Three key words: Delight, Beauty and Gift' a useful framework for doing this.

Alternatively, your group might prefer to read some or all of the pages for themselves.

Read
Genesis 1.1 – 2.3 (Contemporary English Version– CEV)

Because this passage is quite long and very familiar you might like to divide it into seven 'day' sections, as suggested, and read it aloud with several voices. (Make sure you give people time to prepare this in advance.) Alternatively, give people time to read the passage silently to themselves.

> [Reader 1]
> ¹In the beginning God created the heavens and the earth. ²The earth was barren, with no form of life; it was under a roaring ocean covered with darkness. But the Spirit of God was moving over the water.
>
> ³God said, 'I command light to shine!' And light started shining. ⁴God looked at the light and saw that it was good. He separated light from darkness ⁵and named the light 'Day' and the darkness 'Night'. Evening came and then morning – that was the first day.

[Reader 2]
⁶God said, 'I command a dome to separate the water above it from the water below it.' ⁷And that's what happened. God made the dome ⁸and named it 'Sky'. Evening came and then morning – that was the second day.

[Reader 3]
⁹God said, 'I command the water under the sky to come together in one place, so there will be dry ground.' And that's what happened. ¹⁰God named the dry ground 'Land', and he named the water 'Ocean'. God looked at what he had done and saw that it was good.

¹¹God said, 'I command the earth to produce all kinds of plants, including fruit trees and grain.' And that's what happened. ¹²The earth produced all kinds of vegetation. God looked at what he had done, and it was good. ¹³Evening came and then morning – that was the third day.

[Reader 4]
¹⁴God said, 'I command lights to appear in the sky and to separate day from night and to show the time for seasons, special days, and years. ¹⁵I command them to shine on the earth.' And that's what happened. ¹⁶God made two powerful lights, the brighter one to rule the day and the other to rule the night. He also made the stars. ¹⁷Then God put these lights in the sky to shine on the earth, ¹⁸to rule day and night, and to separate light from darkness. God looked at what he had done, and it was good. ¹⁹Evening came and then morning – that was the fourth day.

[Reader 5]
²⁰God said, 'I command the ocean to be full of living creatures, and I command birds to fly above the earth.' ²¹So God made the giant sea monsters and all the living creatures that swim in the ocean. He also made every kind of bird. God looked at what he had done, and it was good. ²²Then he gave the living creatures

his blessing – he told the ocean creatures to live everywhere in the ocean and the birds to live everywhere on earth. [23]Evening came and then morning – that was the fifth day.

[Reader 6]
[24]God said, 'I command the earth to give life to all kinds of tame animals, wild animals, and reptiles.' And that's what happened. [25]God made every one of them. Then he looked at what he had done, and it was good.

[26]God said, 'Now we will make humans, and they will be like us. We will let them rule the fish, the birds, and all other living creatures.'

[27]So God created humans to be like himself; he made men and women. [28]God gave them his blessing and said:

Have a lot of children! Fill the earth with people and bring it under your control. Rule over the fish in the ocean, the birds in the sky, and every animal on the earth.

[29]I have provided all kinds of fruit and grain for you to eat. [30]And I have given the green plants as food for everything else that breathes. These will be food for animals, both wild and tame, and for birds.

[31]God looked at what he had done. All of it was very good! Evening came and then morning – that was the sixth day.

[Reader 7]
[1]So the heavens and the earth and everything else were created.

[2]By the seventh day God had finished his work, and so he rested. [3]God blessed the seventh day and made it special because on that day he rested from his work.

Philippians 4.4-6 (NRSV)

[4] Rejoice in the Lord always; again I will say, Rejoice. [5] Let your gentleness be known to everyone. The Lord is near. [6] Do not worry about anything, but in everything by prayer and supplication with thanksgiving let your requests be made known to God.

>>Talk about it (20 minutes)

Consider some or all of the following questions:

> 'God looked . . . and it was good.' How much of your conversation focuses on the good things in your life rather than the niggles and complaints? How could you learn new habits of thankfulness?

> What *one* thing do you most want to celebrate about your journey of faith in Christ?

> What *one* vital element of modern living would you miss most if it were not available? Do you take this thing for granted? Are there things you could do that might make this thing available to people who don't have it?

> In what way will 'celebrating the good' cause you to 'go against the flow' amongst those with whom you live and work?

> What are the benefits of living in the present moment?

> Are experiences of corporate worship in your church times of delight and celebration?

*Jesus focus

Read the story of Jesus and the woman at Bethany in Mark 14.3-9.

What does Jesus' response to this woman's gesture tell us about Sabbath attitudes of celebration and living in the present?

>>*Do something [10 minutes]

Invite group members each to make a list of five things –
their best view, best sound, best smell, best taste and best
physical sensation (e.g. stroking their pet dog, paddling in cold sea,
walking on snow, sitting on warm sand).

Share your lists together. If you have time you might like to share food
together and read out your 'Best Things' as you eat. ('Table Songs' –
songs and poems of celebration during meals – are part of the Jewish
Sabbath tradition!) Alternatively, you could arrange to go out to eat
together in the near future – perhaps agreeing to bring your 'Best
Things' lists with you.

>>Get Real! – Celebration time
[5 minutes]

Choose one or more of the following suggestions for building
celebration into our everyday lives and encourage the group to try out at
least one of them before the next session. (If you and your group have
suggestions of your own then go with your own ideas.) You might want
to put the suggestions to the group and agree a shared activity or
common focus, or you might prefer to give group members the freedom
to pursue an individual project or course of action.

> Psalm 92 is a Sabbath Psalm of celebration – '. . . at
the works of your hands I sing for joy' (Psalm 92.4, NRSV).
Write your own psalm of celebration.

> Go for a walk or sit still somewhere during the week –
notice all the things that give you joy and make a point of
celebrating them.

> Make a point of turning frustrating waiting times (queuing,
waiting for the kettle to boil, or the lights to change or the
computer to boot up) into reflective moments where you
appreciate all the things you take for granted.

> In your Sabbath notebook make a list of either your 'Seven
wonders of the world', your 'These are a few of my favourite
things', your 'Reasons to be cheerful' or some of the good
things in the life you take for granted. Bring these to the
next session to share with others.

>>Go deep . . . (15 minutes)

Create a still atmosphere. You could light a candle or play some music.

Choose some of the following activities as appropriate to your group:

> Watch a clip from the film *Chariots of Fire*. Introduce the extract with the following information and follow it with a few moments of silent reflection:

Scottish Presbyterian preacher and former Scotland rugby player Eric Liddell is chosen to run in the 1924 Olympic Games in Paris. His sister Jenny, who, with Liddell runs a mission church in Edinburgh, fears that running is diverting Eric from his calling to be a missionary in China. Eric tells her that his vocation is unchanged but that he believes it is also part of God's purpose for him to run. He says to Jenny, 'God made me fast, and when I run I feel his pleasure.'

When Liddell, a strict observer of the Sabbath, discovers that his Olympic 100 m heat is on a Sunday, he refuses to take part. Entered instead – at short notice – for the 400 m, Liddell goes on to win a gold medal.

If using video, watch from 1.47.17 (when the crowds are gathering for the 400 m final) until 1.51.45 (Eric's victory celebrations) – a four-and-a-half-minute clip. If using DVD, start at the beginning of Scene 22 and watch until Liddell makes a victory gesture to Jenny – a four-minute clip. If you have time, you could also watch Eric and Jenny's conversation about his vocation – Scene 10 of the DVD or 53.50 (Eric's late arrival at the Mission) to 57.36 (the end of their conversation on Arthur's Seat – an additional four minute clip.

> Sing 'Come on and Celebrate' (*Mission Praise: Combined*, 99).

> Read Psalm 92.1-5.

> Make a celebration collage:
Place a large sheet of sugar paper or part of a roll of lining paper in the middle of the group along with PVA glue and a

selection of collage materials such as feathers, coloured sand, pot pourri, torn tissue paper, images cut from magazines, sequins, foil shapes, wool, or scraps of fabric. Invite people to glue things on to represent things in their lives they feel good about.

> Use this exercise based on Gerard Hughes, *God of Surprises*, p. 78. Invite group members to sit comfortably and close their eyes and then lead them slowly through this contemplative exercise.

Think back over your day.

Let your mind wander (without any self-judgement – be it approval or disapproval) and bring into focus anything for which you are grateful . . .

This might be an enjoyable experience, a specific achievement, a kind word given or received, the sight of a raindrop or the very fact that you can see at all. Often these moments go unnoticed or are quickly forgotten or obscured by the more painful experiences of the day.

Relive these moments or experiences now . . .

Bring them to mind and relish them.

(Pause)

What were your moods and feelings in these moments?

(Pause)

Now praise and thank God for all that was good about your day.

Pray

Use one or more of the following prayers or pray in your own words.

For the glory of creation
Celebrate and dance.
For tenderness and joy
Celebrate and dance.
For all we take for granted
Celebrate and dance.
For beauty and discovery
Celebrate and dance.
For the gift of Christ Jesus
Celebrate and dance.

For the miracle of life
Celebrate and dance.

Dear God
Thank you that you delight in us.
Thank you for the beauty of the earth.
Thank you for the gift of love.
Amen.
Sunsets and spangled seas,
birdsong and humming bees,
mountains and mighty trees
God saw that it was good.

Crashing waves and waterfalls,
sunlight on mossy walls,
children throwing snowballs
God saw that it was good.

Juice dripping from a peach,
walking on an empty beach,
laughter and human speech
God saw that it was good.

Babies' skin and dogs' fur,
the comfort of a cat's purr,
seasons and the turning year
God saw that it was good.

Fresh-cut grass and apple pies,
daffodils and dragonflies,
wild moors and lark's rise
God saw that it was good.

A lover's smile, a helping hand,
elephants, a brass band,
burying your toes in sand!
God saw that it was good.

>>Aim

This session aims to explore what it means to rest and to consider themes of grace and restoration in the light of biblical teaching about Sabbath.

What you will need (make your own selection)

> *candles;
> *music to help focus on Sabbath rest (see page 11 for suggestions);
> *objects to provide a visual focus (see page 12);
> A4 paper and pens;
> *songbooks;
> *video or DVD of *The Mission* (see page 69).

>>Background

Leaders: please see pages 7–8 for tips on how to use this material.

Three key words

Restoration, Remembrance, Grace

1 Restoration

> A second meaning of the Hebrew word 'Shabbat' is 'to rest', both mentally and physically.
> The Sabbath instructions in Deuteronomy 5 require a complete cessation of work for the whole community – family, servants, neighbours and even animals.
> Rest is more than just relaxation or a break from work. Rest is about recovery and restoration. In 1 Kings 19.4-8, Elijah's depleted reserves are replenished by sleep, food and drink.

The Hebrew word for rest, 'menuha', means held or embraced like a child at its mother's breast.

In the tempestuous ocean of time and toil there are islands of stillness where man may enter a harbour and reclaim his dignity. The island is the seventh day, the Sabbath, a day of detachment from things, instruments and practical affairs as well as of attachment to the spirit.

Abraham Joshua Heschel, The Sabbath, *p. 29*

2 Remembrance

> Deuteronomy 5 links Sabbath keeping with remembering God's deliverance of the people of Israel from slavery in Egypt.

> In the ritual that marks the start of the Sabbath in a Jewish home, two 'Kiddush' candles are lit, one for 'observe' and the other for 'remember'. Remembrance of all God has done is an essential part of Sabbath rest.

> Resting reminds us that all that we have and all that we are come from God and that he is the author and perfecter of our faith, the Lord of our lives, the potter moulding clay.

The spiritual rest which God especially intends . . . is that we not only cease from labour and trade but much more – that we let God alone work in us and that in all our powers do we nothing of our own.

Martin Luther, quoted by Marva J. Dawn
in Keeping the Sabbath Wholly, *p. 52*

3 Grace

> The Sabbath is the *first* day of the week – not the 'week end'. It is meant to sustain us, *not* reward us for working hard all week!

> Grace is the underlying dynamic of the Sabbath. God's love for us doesn't depend on what we do. *Receiving* God's love is fundamental in being a follower of Christ.

> Proper rest will, most likely, make our work more effective but that is not its primary purpose. This runs contrary to the 'Protestant work ethic' that has pervaded and shaped our culture for the past 500 years. True Sabbath elevates rest, play and celebration above work and productivity. We are human *beings*, not human *doings*.

To be fully alive involves being open to the renewable resources of creation, human society and grace that are given to sustain life. Being human, then, begins with *grace* and with the ability to live in *thanksgiving* out of the 'renewable resources' which life opens up to us.

Robert Warren, Being Human, Being Church, *p. 118*

Sabbath attitudes of receiving and giving rest help us order our priorities and recognize our dependence on God's goodness.

Cutting across

. . . activism and the need to appear busy;
. . . acquisitiveness and the drive to achieve;
. . . a tendency to define ourselves in terms of the job we do – and to ask people on first meeting them 'What do you *do*?'
. . . human greed and the desire to have domination over the earth, its people and its resources;
. . . an inability to stop and a fear of doing nothing!

A folk tale tells of two men who chopped wood for a whole day. One man chopped constantly without a break. The second rested for ten minutes in every hour. At the end of the day it was the second man who had chopped more wood. Puzzled by this, the first man asked his colleague how this could be. 'It's simple,' said the second man. 'Whenever I rested, I sharpened my axe.'

Man is not a beast of burden, and the Sabbath is not for the purpose of enhancing the efficiency of his work.

Heschel, The Sabbath and its Meaning for Modern Man, *p. 14*

>> 3 Time to Rest/The Session

>>Welcome (10 minutes)

Introduction

Welcome people back to the group and explain that this
session considers the theme of Sabbath rest.

Pray

Create a still atmosphere. As this session is about resting and being
still, spend a little longer than usual on this.

You might like to light a candle, play some music or encourage people
to focus on something that symbolizes Sabbath rest (see pages 11–12
for suggestions). Alternatively, provide a visual resource such as a cross
or image of Christ (see ideas on page 13).

One of the following actions may be helpful:
> Invite group members to clench their fists and then slowly
  open their hands, placing them palm upwards as a sign that
  they are letting go of tensions and anxieties and opening
  themselves to receiving peace and refreshment.
> Provide some large pebbles – one each – and suggest that
  group members first cradle a stone and then lay it down as a
  symbol of their desire to lay down all that makes them heavy
  and weary, in readiness to receive Christ's rest.

Now pray in your own words, asking God to help you as you meet
together, or use the Course Prayer.

Course Prayer

God of eternity, teach us to pause.
God of creation, teach us to wonder.
God of Sabbath, teach us to rest.
God of delight, teach us to play.
God of the poor, teach us to share in your work of liberation.

God of love, reconciling us through Christ Jesus,
fill our lives with your perfect peace. Amen.

>>*Action replay (10 minutes)

Invite group members to talk about the things they did during
the week as a result of the *Get Real!* part of the last session.
Allow time for people to share snippets from their Sabbath notebooks
if they have been keeping them.

>>*Brainstorm (5 minutes)

*What's the most restful place you've ever been to? What makes
it restful?*

Share your answers in pairs or with the whole group.

>>*Do something (5 minutes)

Invite the group to sit comfortably and listen to a relaxing
piece of music. (See page 11 for ideas of music to use.)

>>Encounter (15 minutes)

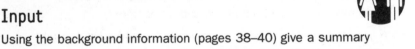

Input

Using the background information (pages 38–40) give a summary
of its ideas about Sabbath rest. You might find the 'Three key words:
Restoration, Remembrance and Grace' a useful framework for doing this.

Alternatively, your group might prefer to read some or all of the pages
for themselves.

Read
Deuteronomy 5.12-15 (NRSV)

> [12] Observe the sabbath day and keep it holy, as the Lord your God
> commanded you. [13] For six days you shall labour and do all your
> work. [14] But the seventh day is a sabbath to the Lord your God;

you shall not do any work – you, or your son or your daughter, or your male slave or female slave, or your ox or your donkey, or any of your livestock, or the resident alien in your towns, so that your male and female slave may rest as well as you. ¹⁵ Remember that you were a slave in the land of Egypt, and the Lord your God brought you out from there with a mighty hand and an outstretched arm; therefore the Lord your God commanded you to keep the sabbath day.

*1 Kings 19.4-8 (NRSV)

⁴[Elijah] went a day's journey into the wilderness, and came and sat down under a solitary broom tree. He asked that he might die: 'It is enough; now, O Lord, take away my life, for I am no better than my ancestors.' ⁵Then he lay down under the broom tree and fell asleep. Suddenly an angel touched him and said to him, 'Get up and eat.' ⁶He looked, and there at his head was a cake baked on hot stones, and a jar of water. He ate and drank, and lay down again. ⁷The angel of the Lord came a second time, touched him and said, 'Get up and eat, otherwise the journey will be too much for you.' ⁸He got up, and ate and drank; then he went in the strength of that food for forty days and forty nights.

Matthew 11.28 (NRSV)

Come to me, all you that are weary and are carrying heavy burdens, and I will give you rest.

>>Talk about it (25 minutes)

Consider some of or all the following questions:

> What is the link between Sabbath rest and the memory of slavery in Deuteronomy 5?

> Is rest the same as relaxation?

> What does it mean to keep something 'holy'?

> In what ways (if any) are you a 'slave driver'?

> What do Sabbath rest principles have to say to our society's values and working practices?

> High achieving, hardworking people are often called 'driven'. What attitudes characterize 'driven' people and how do these differ from 'Sabbath attitudes'?

> What is your response to the story of how Elijah is looked after in 1 Kings 19?

> What kind of rest does Jesus promise us in Matthew 11.28? Does this connect with your experience?

*Jesus focus

Read the story of Jesus at the home of Martha and Mary in Luke 10.38-42.

In this episode, Jesus gently rebukes Martha's scrambled priorities and offers her the radically liberating alternative of stillness, company and 'being'.

How do you imagine Mary and Martha felt after this encounter with Jesus?

>>Get real! (5 minutes)

Do something practical this week to give someone else the gift of Sabbath rest. This could be:

> cooking a meal for somebody;

> babysitting for busy parents so they can have some time off;

> providing refreshments for a team of people working long hours on a project;

> doing some driving for someone who normally spends a lot of time behind the wheel (perhaps doing school pick-ups or drop-offs);

> spending time with somebody who needs constant care so that his or her carer can have a break.

Either organize these 'Sabbath gifts' as a group or agree to do things individually.

>>Go deep . . . (15 minutes)

Create a still atmosphere again. You could light a candle or play some music.

Choose some of the following activities as appropriate to your group:

> **Watch** a clip from the film *The Mission*. Introduce the film with the following information and follow it with a moment of silence to reflect on the scene you have just watched:

Rodrigo Mendoza (Robert De Niro), a former mercenary and slave trader who has murdered his brother in a duel, is challenged by a Jesuit priest (Jeremy Irons) to go with a group of brothers to establish a mission church amongst an indigenous tribe in 1750s' Latin America. During their arduous journey through mountainous rainforest and up the sheer cliff face of a waterfall, Mendoza chooses to carry a net full of heavy metal armour, as a penance for his past life. Weighed down and exhausted by his burden, Mendoza is finally released from guilt when a young Indian boy cuts the rope to send the armour crashing downhill.

Either start the video at 28.42 (the start of Jeremy Irons' conversation in Mendoza's cell – Scene 9 on the DVD) and play through to 41.40 (the end of the scene where Mendoza's burden is released) – a fourteen-minute clip

or

Start at 35.43, immediately after Jeremy Irons' line 'We're not the members of a democracy, Father. We're members of an order. . .' (Part way through Scene 10 on the DVD) and finish (as above) at 41.40 – a six-minute clip.

> **Listen** to the song 'He's got the whole world in his hands' (there is a wonderful version by Nina Simone – see page 11 for details). As you listen, picture yourself and your family and friends resting in God's arms.

> **Sing** 'Be still, for the presence of the Lord' (*Mission Praise: Combined*, 50).

> **Read** Psalm 46.10.

> **Sit** comfortably in complete silence for five minutes.

Pray

Use one or more of the following prayers or pray in your own words:

Managers, commuters,
workers stuck behind computers . . .
**Lay your burdens down,
come to me and rest.**
Labourers on the soil,
all who dig and sweat and toil . . .
**Lay your burdens down,
come to me and rest.**
Overstretched and overstressed,
underpaid, abused, oppressed . . .
**Lay your burdens down,
come to me and rest.**
Unemployed or long-term ill,
those with too much time to fill . . .
**Lay your burdens down,
come to me and rest.**
In the home, on the road,
those with dangerous overload . . .
**Lay your burdens down,
come to me and rest.**
Those who never get a break,
those who give while others take . . .
**Lay your burdens down,
come to me and rest**.

Loving God, refresh us.
Healing God, restore us.
Mighty God, remake us.
Gracious God, renew us.
Amen.

May Christ, the bread of life,
nourish your soul;
may Christ, healer of the nations,
make you whole;
may Christ, who broke the chains of sin,
give you rest;
may Christ, the King of kings,
receive you as his guest;
and may Christ, Immanuel, God with us,
give you peace.
Amen.

Sabbath God,
help us to stop,
let go,
cease striving
and rest. Amen.

>>Aim

This session aims to explore what it means to play, be creative and become 'like little children'.

What you will need (make your own selection)

> *candles;
> *music (see page 11 for suggestions);
> *objects to provide a visual focus (see page 12);
> *board game (see page 54 for suggestions);
> *'messy materials' (see page 55 for suggestions);
> *video or DVD of *Amélie* (see Filmography, page 69);
> *picture book *Jesus' Day Off* by Nicholas Allan (see Bibliography, page 69);
> *clay or playdough (see recipe, page 13);
> *collections of multi-sensory objects (see page 56 for suggestions).

>>Background

Leaders: please see pages 7–8 for tips on how to use this material.

Three key words

Creativity, Laughter, Children

1 Creativity

> God himself rested on the Sabbath in order to enjoy and engage with his creation. A surfer's bumper sticker wittily suggests that 'On the seventh day God went windsurfing!'

> God relates to his creation with playfulness and spontaneity. Several of Jesus' parables (e.g. The Prodigal Son (Luke 15.11-32) and The Great Banquet (Luke 14.7-24) picture God as a lavish party-giver.

> The playwright Dennis Potter in his last TV interview before his death from cancer in 1994 described his understanding of God as 'the feeling of there being something to sing and dance about'.

Our understanding of creativity is distorted today by our consumer culture and by the notion that 'creativity' is what we do in our 'leisure time'. However, to be human is to be creative and we need to practise – and help others experience – the essential creativity at the heart of all we do and are. Parents, plumbers, teachers, those who work in factories or offices, politicians, athletes, clergy are *all* engaged in creativity.

Adapted from Robert Warren, Being Human, Being Church, *pp. 121–2*

---

2 Laughter

> The booming leisure industry suggests that our time-driven society is waking up to the fact that fun is good for us. (Many families apparently now spend more on recreation each week than they do on food!) Play and leisure are seen as essential to well-being and it has been scientifically proven that laughter is good for us.

> Laughter puts us in touch with our deepest humanity and joins us to each other.

> Play and laughter can sustain us through dark and difficult experiences.

Brian Keenan, while in captivity, in the midst of sustained, dehumanizing maltreatment, found himself laughing with other prisoners. Later, he wrote:

There are many things a man can resist – pain, torture, loss of loved ones – but laughter ultimately he cannot resist.

Brian Keenan, An Evil Cradling, *p. 269*

It is pleasing to God whenever thou rejoicest or laughest from the bottom of thy heart.

If I am not allowed to laugh in heaven, I don't want to go there.

Martin Luther

3 Children

In Matthew 18.1-4 Jesus encourages us to become like little children.

> Children are spontaneous and full of wonder and delight.

> Children enquire and explore: they do not think they 'know it all' or 'have seen it all'. They are curious and hungry for life.

> Children are relatively carefree. They often display the same absence of worry shared by the 'birds of the air' and the 'lilies of the field' – commended by Jesus in Matthew 6.25-34.

Children have the capacity to live in the moment and to enjoy life as a gift rather than handle it as some problem to be solved. This may well be why Christ placed a child in the middle of the disciples when he was teaching them about how to *receive* the kingdom.

Adapted from Robert Warren, Being Human, Being Church, *p. 118*

Martin Luther encouraged clergy to spend time with little children and with animals and 'all that takes life blithely'.

Robert Warren, Living Well, *p. 37*

Rediscovering how to play and becoming childlike (not child-*ish*) in our approach to life puts us in touch with many secrets of the kingdom of God.

Cutting across

. . . weariness and deadness of spirit;

. . . apathy and cynicism;

. . . excessive self-importance;

. . . overvaluing of work and productivity;

. . . self-justification and self-sufficiency;

. . . anxiety and self-pity.

Joy is the serious business of heaven.

C. S. Lewis, Letters to Malcolm, *p. 122*

>>Welcome (10 minutes)

Introduction

Welcome people back to the group and explain that this session considers the theme of Sabbath play.

Pray

Create a still atmosphere. You might like to light a candle, play some music or encourage people to focus on something that symbolizes Sabbath play (see page 12 for suggestions). Alternatively, provide a visual resource such as a cross or image of Christ (see ideas on page 13).

Pray in your own words, asking God to help you as you meet together, or use the Course Prayer.

> #### Course Prayer
>
> God of eternity, teach us to pause.
> God of creation, teach us to wonder.
> God of Sabbath, teach us to rest.
> God of delight, teach us to play.
> God of the poor, teach us to share in your work of liberation.
> God of love, reconciling us through Christ Jesus,
> fill our lives with your perfect peace. Amen.

>>*Action replay (10 minutes)

Invite group members to talk about the things they did during the week as a result of the *Get Real!* part of the last session. Allow time for people to share snippets from their Sabbath notebooks if they are keeping them.

>>*Brainstorm (5 minutes)

How and where did you play as a child?

Share anecdotes of favourite childhood games, toys, haunts or pleasures.

>>Encounter (15 minutes)

Input

Using the background information (pages 48–51) give a summary of its ideas about Sabbath play. You might find the 'Three key words: Creativity, Laughter and Children' a useful framework for doing this.

Alternatively, your group might prefer to read some or all of the pages for themselves.

Read
Isaiah 11.6-9 (NRSV)

> [6] The wolf shall live with the lamb,
>   the leopard shall lie down with the kid,
> the calf and the lion and the fatling together,
>   and a little child shall lead them.
> [7] The cow and the bear shall graze,
>   their young shall lie down together;
> and the lion shall eat straw like the ox.
> [8] The nursing child shall play over the hole of an asp,
>   and the weaned child shall put its hand on the adder's den.
> [9] They will not hurt or destroy
>   on all my holy mountain;
> for the earth will be full of the knowledge of the Lord
>   as the waters cover the sea.

Matthew 18.1-5 (NRSV)

> [1] At that time the disciples came to Jesus and asked, 'Who is the greatest in the kingdom of heaven?' [2] He called a child, whom he put among them, [3] and said, 'Truly I tell you, unless you change and become like children, you will never enter the kingdom of heaven. [4] Whoever becomes humble like this child is the greatest in the kingdom of heaven. [5] Whoever welcomes one such child in my name welcomes me.'

>>Talk about it (20 minutes)

Consider some of or all the following questions:

> What are children like and why does Jesus value them so highly?

> How much time each week do you spend playing? (Look back at your pie chart from Session 1.) If you don't play at all, when and how did you last experience play?

> What most makes you laugh? Are there things that Christians should *not* laugh at?

> When, where and how do you feel you are at your most creative?

> Martin Luther recommended spending time with animals, children and all that 'takes life blithely'. What do you think he meant and do you agree?

> Look back at your list of 'Sabbath Attitudes' from Session 1. Are there any qualities you want to add to it in the light of this session?

> 'Too easily in the church it is all work, all form, all order: we have lost the freedom, the play and the ability to enjoy God, life, each other, creation and the present moment.' (*Emmaus: Your Kingdom Come*, p. 89.) Is this true of your church?

---

*Jesus focus

Read about Jesus and his disciples snatching some precious time together in Mark 6.30-32.

What do you suppose Jesus and his friends did in the boat on their way to the deserted place?

>>Do something (15 minutes)

Either:

> Play a game together, e.g. *Uno*, *Pictionary* or *Jenga*;

or

> do something playful and creative such as clay modelling,
  collage, finger painting or icing biscuits. (You might like to ask
  the people who work with your church's children's groups to
  give you some messy ideas!)

>>Get real! (5 minutes)

In the coming week think about how you can build more play
into your daily, weekly or monthly rhythm.

Resolve to do something 'playful' in the coming days. Ideas might
include:

> flying a kite;

> sailing a boat;

> baking a cake;

> looking more closely at flowers or birds;

> playing a neglected musical instrument;

> taking up (or reviving) a creative hobby;

> lying on the grass or walking along a wall!

You might like to get together and do some of these things as a group.

>>Go deep . . . (10 minutes)

Create a playful atmosphere. You could play some upbeat
music such as jazz or salsa music (see page 11 for ideas),
provide a colourful focus of flowers or fruit for people to look at,
or eat a tasty snack together.

Choose some of the following activities as appropriate to your group:

> Watch the opening sequence of the French film *Amélie*. You
  might like to introduce it with the following information:

*Amélie Poulain – a six-year-old girl at the start of the film – has a
child's sense of wonder and play and a quirky sense of humour.
The opening credits show Amélie pulling faces and playing
spontaneously with a series of objects.*

If you are watching on video start one minute into the film (after the birth of the baby) and run the film for 1 minute 40 seconds (until the doctor in a white coat appears). If you are using DVD, watch Scene 1 from 1.33 to 3.12. As this is such a short sequence you might like to show it a second time. Follow the clip with a few moments for silent reflection on the spirit of playfulness that the clip captures.

> Read the children's picture book *Jesus' Day Off* by Nicholas Allan. Spend some moments (perhaps while music plays) playing with clay or playdough (see recipe on page 13). Give each group member his or her own piece to fiddle with. You could use the following prayer to introduce or conclude this activity:

Lord of texture and touch,
of softness, warmth and movement,
thank you that you moulded us from clay,
took delight in us
and gave us the instinct to share your creative work.
Set us free to enjoy as you enjoy
and to receive the gift of life in all its fullness.
Amen.

> Read Matthew 6.25-34.

> Hand round a series of objects that feel, smell or look nice. (Choose about six things, such as a feather, a shell, a flower, an orange, a furry soft toy, a sprig of rosemary, a bowl of jelly, a tomato cut in half, a lavender bag . . . the possibilities are endless!) Invite group members to handle the objects silently, reverently and using their senses. Introduce or conclude this activity with the following prayer:

For fur and feathers, frogs and flamingos
Thank you, playful God.
For shells and sunflowers, starlight and smells
Thank you, playful God.

For puddles and pomegranates, peacocks and plums
Thank you, playful God.
For giraffes and guinea pigs, jelly and jokes
Thank you, playful God.
For all that is squashy, squelchy, sparkly or soft
Thank you, playful God.
For your wiggly, wobbly, wonderful world
Thank you, playful God. Amen.

Pray

Use one or more of the following prayers or pray in your own words.

God, who knit me together in my mother's womb,
weave threads of joy and abundance through my life;
God, who makes trees clap their hands and mountains
burst into song,
flood my days with laughter and dancing;
God, who came to earth as a defenceless baby,
give me the trust and openness of a child;
and may Christ, the source of living water,
make my life a bubbling spring.
Amen.

Creative God,
create community where there is isolation,
create possibilities where there is lack of hope,
create bridges where there are only stone walls,
create peace where there is bloodshed,
create life where there is death,
create joy where there is sorrow,
create love where there is hatred.
Amen.

>>Aim

This session aims to explore the themes of liberation and jubilee and to revisit some of the themes of previous sessions by way of a conclusion to the course.

What you will need (make your own selection)

> > *candles;
> > *music (see page 11 for suggestions);
> > * objects to provide a visual focus for Sabbath liberation (see page 12);
> > flipchart or large sheet of paper and marker pens;
> > 'brainstorm' sheet about Sabbath from Session 1;
> > group members' 'pie charts' from Session 1;
> > *video or DVD of *The Shawshank Redemption* (see Filmography, page 69);
> > A4 paper and pens;
> > *songbooks.

>>Background:

Leaders: please see pages 7–8 for tips on how to use this material.

Three key words

Freedom, Jubilee, Resolution

1 Freedom

> > Liberation is fundamental to Jesus' ministry – Luke 4.14-21. Jesus quotes from Isaiah 61, establishing that the liberation of captives and the bringing of good news to the poor will be fundamental to his ministry.

> Liberation is at the heart of Sabbath. In Luke 13.10-17 Jesus liberates a crippled woman from physical bondage and the stigma of disfigurement. When criticized by the synagogue officials for doing this on the Sabbath, Jesus challenges their short-sighted obsession with rules and their failure to grasp that freedom from bondage ('untying') is what Sabbath is all about.

> Jews use the greeting 'Shabbat Shalom' to wish one another peace, wholeness and well-being on the Sabbath.

Man was born free and everywhere he is in chains.

Jean-Jacques Rousseau, Du Contrat Social, *1762*

---

2 Jubilee

> Sabbath is for the well-being of whole communities and the land as well. Sabbath principles affect farming, working practices, family life, the treatment of the poor and issues of justice and peace.

> The laws concerning Sabbath in Leviticus 25 established a one-year-in-seven rhythm of agricultural practice that both rests the land and provides for the marginalized in society during this 'Sabbath year'.

> The jubilee principle extends this pattern further – after seven sets of seven-year cycles (49 years) there is to be a fiftieth, jubilee year (named after the Hebrew trumpet or *yobel* that would announce its arrival) when land will be left fallow, slaves freed, debts cancelled and property restored.

> The jubilee mission of the Church is to feed the hungry, clothe the naked and visit those in prison (Matthew 25.31-40) as well as to rise above prejudices of race, class, gender or appearance in order to do so (James 2.1-6).

> Isaiah 58.13,14 links honouring the Sabbath with choosing to act unselfishly. Sabbath keeping leads to justice keeping, which leads to peace keeping.

Sabbath keeping exposes our political illusions. To think about God and the lifestyle to which he calls us forces us to see that our political power plays do not accomplish God's purposes . . . Instead of scrambling for war and military aggression, we must relearn the values of cooperation and sharing, of non-violence and support.

Marva J. Dawn, Keeping the Sabbath Wholly, *p. 93*

3 Resolution

> In the Millennium year, much was made of the principle of jubilee with the Jubilee 2000 campaign calling for the cancellation of debt in the world's poorest countries. Governments were asked to 'break the chains of debt'. The momentum of this campaign and 'Make Poverty History' (launched in 2005), and the growing awareness of fair trade issues have put Sabbath principles of liberation and Shalom on society's agenda.

> The Millennium Resolution adopted by the Christian Church in 2000 reinforced this commitment to Sabbath principles:

Let there be
respect for the earth,
peace for its people,
love in our lives,
delight in the good,
forgiveness of past wrongs
and from now on a new start.

The gap between the world's rich and poor has never been wider. Malnutrition, AIDS, conflict and illiteracy are a daily reality for millions. But it isn't chance or bad luck that keeps people trapped in bitter, unrelenting poverty. It's man-made factors like a glaringly unjust global trade system, a debt burden so great that it suffocates any chance of recovery and insufficient and ineffective aid.

Make Poverty History web site, April 2005

Taking responsibility for the Sabbath liberation of others will challenge our lifestyle and values.

Cutting across

. . . self-interest;

. . . oppressive political and economic regimes and practices that 'tie people up';

. . . a shallow definition of rest and relaxation as private, individualistic pursuits;

. . . religious observance with no social conscience.

>>Welcome (10 minutes)

Introduction

Welcome people back to the group. Explain that this session considers the theme of Sabbath liberation and also reflects back over the previous four sessions.

Pray

Create a still atmosphere. You might like to light a candle, play some music or encourage people to focus on something that symbolizes Sabbath liberation (see page 12 for suggestions). Alternatively, provide a visual resource such as a cross or image of Christ (see ideas on page 13).

Pray in your own words, asking God to help you as you meet together, or use the Course Prayer.

Course Prayer

God of eternity, teach us to pause.
God of creation, teach us to wonder.
God of Sabbath, teach us to rest.
God of delight, teach us to play.
God of the poor, teach us to share in your work of liberation.
God of love, reconciling us through Christ Jesus,
fill our lives with your perfect peace. Amen.

>>*Action replay (10 minutes)

Invite group members to talk about the things they did during the week as a result of the *Get Real!* part of the last session. Allow time for people to share snippets from their Sabbath notebooks if they are keeping them.

>>*Brainstorm (5 minutes)

What things give human beings a sense of well-being?

Make a list together as a group or in pairs and share your ideas with each other.

>>Encounter (15 minutes)
Input

Using the background information (pages 58–61) give a summary of its ideas about Sabbath liberation. You might find the 'Three key words: Freedom, Jubilee and Resolution' a useful framework for doing this.

Alternatively, your group might prefer to read some of or all the pages for themselves.

Read
Leviticus 25.1-12 (NRSV)

¹ The Lord spoke to Moses on Mount Sinai, saying: ² 'Speak to the people of Israel and say to them: When you enter the land that I am giving you, the land shall observe a sabbath for the Lord. ³ For six years you shall sow your field, and for six years you shall prune your vineyard, and gather in their yield; ⁴ but in the seventh year there shall be a sabbath of complete rest for the land, a sabbath for the Lord: you shall not sow your field or prune your vineyard. ⁵ You shall not reap the aftergrowth of your harvest or gather the grapes of your unpruned vine: it shall be a year of complete rest for the land. ⁶ You may eat what the land yields during its sabbath – you, your male and female slaves, your hired and your bound labourers who live with you; ⁷ for your livestock also, and for the wild animals in your land all its yield shall be for food.

⁸ 'You shall count off seven weeks of years, seven times seven years, so that the period of seven weeks of years gives forty-nine years. ⁹ Then you shall have the trumpet sounded loud; on the tenth day of the seventh month – on the day of atonement – you shall have the trumpet sounded throughout all your land. ¹⁰ And you shall hallow the fiftieth year and you shall proclaim liberty

throughout the land to all its inhabitants. It shall be a jubilee for you: you shall return, every one of you to your family. ¹¹ That fiftieth year shall be a jubilee for you: you shall not sow, or reap the aftergrowth, or harvest the unpruned vines. ¹² For it is a jubilee; it shall be holy to you: you shall eat only what the field itself produces.'

Luke 13.10-17 (CEV)

¹⁰ One Sabbath, Jesus was teaching in a Jewish meeting place, ¹¹and a woman was there who had been crippled by an evil spirit for 18 years. She was completely bent over and couldn't straighten up. ¹² When Jesus saw the woman, he called her over and said, 'You are now well.' ¹³ He placed his hands on her, and at once she stood up straight and praised God.

¹⁴ The man in charge of the meeting place was angry because Jesus had healed someone on the Sabbath. So he said to the people, 'Each week has six days when we can work. Come and be healed on one of those days, but not on the Sabbath.'

¹⁵ The Lord replied, 'Are you trying to fool someone! Won't any one of you untie your bullock or donkey and lead it out to drink on a Sabbath? ¹⁶ This woman belongs to the family of Abraham, but Satan has kept her bound for 18 years. Isn't it right to set her free on the Sabbath?' ¹⁷Jesus' words made his enemies ashamed. But everyone else in the crowd was happy about the wonderful things he was doing.

>>Talk about it (20 minutes)

Consider some or all of the following questions:

> What do you think of the idea of jubilee described in Leviticus 25.10-12?

> Isaiah 58.13,14 commands Israel to refrain from the pursuit of self-interest on the Sabbath. What might this mean for us, our families and our church?

> Imagine yourself as the woman in the story in Luke 13. What do you think she might have said after this encounter:

   to Jesus?

   to the Pharisees?

> Sabbath principles have global and political implications. What issues concern you in the light of the Bible passages you have just read?

> Looking back at the course as a whole, what Sabbath attitudes have most impressed you?

*Jesus focus

Read Luke 4.14-21.
Jesus quotes these words at the start of his ministry and on the Sabbath.

How does this declaration of intent demonstrate Sabbath principles?

>>*Do something (10 minutes)

As a group, compose your own 'Sabbath Resolution' in the light of all you have discussed and discovered in this and the previous sessions.

>>Get real! (5 minutes)

Look again at the pie chart you drew in Session 1. In the light of all you have discovered about Sabbath during this course, what changes would you like to make in:

> how you spend Sundays or your 'Sabbath' day?

> building in rhythms and routines of rest, play and celebration?

> developing 'Sabbath moments' in everyday life?

> giving Sabbath liberation to others?
   If you would like to do more about the final point, you might want to consider the following actions as individuals or a group:

> Find out more about working practices in the food industry or the clothing industry or about fair trade or debt relief. Resolve to make at least *one* change to your lifestyle or shopping habits as a consequence. The Bibliography (page 69) includes books that may help you.

> Do something practical to bring well-being and liberty to someone in your neighbourhood or further afield.

>>Go deep . . . (15 minutes)

Create a still atmosphere. You could light a candle, play some music or sit silently together. Choose some of the following activities as appropriate to your group:

> **Sing or listen** to 'The Touching Place'.

> **Listen to** 'Travelling the road to freedom' from *A Touching Place*.

> **Listen to** 'The Freedom Samba' from *God in the Flesh* (full details of music on page 12).

> **Watch** a clip from *The Shawshank Redemption*. Introduce the extract with this information, watch the clip, and follow it with a brief period of silence to reflect on what you have watched:

Andy Dufresne – wrongly imprisoned in the unrelentingly brutal Shawshank prison for a murder he didn't commit – serves almost 20 years before effecting a cleverly planned escape that involves gradually tunnelling through the wall of his cell. Emerging through a sewage pipe into the outside world, Andy begins a new life.

If using video, begin at 1.58.35 – the moment when the prison warder discovers Andy's empty cell, and watch up to 2.03.39 (the shot of Andy bare-chested with his arms outstretched) – a five-minute clip. If you are using DVD, watch scene 11, which is six minutes long.

> **Read** this extract from *Long Walk to Freedom* by Nelson Mandela, which describes the events of his release from prison in 1990.

[Leaving prison by car with his wife Winnie, it was suggested by a TV presenter, that Mandela might get out of the car just short of the gate in order to be filmed walking to freedom.]

About a quarter of a mile in front of the gate, the car slowed to a stop and Winnie and I got out and began to walk towards the prison gate. At first I could not really make out what was going on in front of us, but when I was within 150 feet or so, I saw a tremendous commotion and a great crowd of people: hundreds of photographers and television cameras and newspeople as well as several thousand well-wishers. I was astounded and a little bit alarmed. I had truly not expected such a scene . . . When I was among the crowd I raised my fist, and there was a roar. I had not been able to do that for twenty-seven years and it gave me a surge of strength and joy . . .'

[later that day, Mandela was received at City Hall, Capetown]

I walked out on to the balcony and saw a boundless sea of people cheering, holding flags and banners, clapping and laughing. I raised my fist to the crowd, and the crowd responded with an enormous cheer. Those cheers filled me anew with the spirit of the struggle. '*Amandla!*'[1] I called out. '*Ngawethu!*'[2] they responded. '*iAfrika!*' I yelled; '*Mayibuye!*'[3] they answered. Finally, when the crowd had started to settle down, I took out my speech . . .

'Friends, comrades and fellow South Africans. I greet you all in the name of peace, democracy and freedom for all!'

Nelson Mandela, Long Walk to Freedom, *pp. 673, 676*

---

1 In the Nguni languages of South Africa this, roughly translated, means 'power'.
2 Usually means 'to the people' or 'is ours'.
3 In the Sesotho language this means 'our Africa'.

Pray

Use one or more of the following prayers or pray in your own words.

Forgive us Lord when we plunder the earth
All creation groans to be free
Redeem us Lord when we are enslaved by things
All creation groans to be free
Deliver us Lord when we tie ourselves in knots
All creation groans to be free
Heal us Lord when we misuse and abuse your gifts
All creation groans to be free
Have mercy Lord when we trample the poor to become rich
All creation groans to be free
Restore us Lord when we lose sight of each other's worth
All creation groans to be free
Liberate us Lord from all that twists us out of shape
All creation groans to be free

Sabbath God,
set us free,
heal our land,
unleash your Spirit in us.
Amen.

Let justice flow like a river.
Let the desert bloom with peace.
Let the hungry be fed,
the naked be clothed,
the lost be found,
the chained be freed,
and the poor blessed with plenty.
Amen.

>>Bibliography

and Further Resources

Nicholas Allan, *Jesus' Day Off*, Red Fox, 2002.

Bede: *The Reckoning of Time*, [*De Temporum Ratione*], Faith Wallis (trans.), Liverpool University Press, 1999.

Stephen Cottrell, Steven Croft, John Finney, Felicity Lawson and Robert Warren, *Emmaus: Leading an Emmaus Group* and *Emmaus: Your Kingdom Come*, both National Society/Church House Publishing and Bible Society, 1998.

Joy Davidman, *Smoke on the Mountain*, Hodder, 1955.

Marva J. Dawn, *Keeping the Sabbath Wholly*, Eerdmans, 1989.

Abraham Joshua Heschel, *The Sabbath: Its Meaning for Modern Man*, Farrar, Strauss, Giroux, 1951.

Peter Horrobin and Greg Leavers (eds), *Mission Praise: Combined*, Marshall Pickering, 1992.

Gerard Hughes, *God of Surpises*, Darton, Longman & Todd, 1985.

Brian Keenan, *An Evil Cradling*, Vintage, 1993.

Felicity Lawrence, *Not on the Label: What Really Goes into the Food on Your Plate*, Penguin, 2004.

C. S. Lewis, *Letters to Malcolm: Chiefly on Prayer*, Geoffrey Bles, 1964.

Nelson Mandela, *Long Walk to Freedom*, Abacus, 1994.

John O'Donohue, *Divine Beauty – the Invisible Embrace*, Bantam, 2003.

Sara Wenger Shenk, *Why Not Celebrate!*, Good Books, 1987.

Robert Warren, *Being Human, Being Church*, Marshall Pickering, 1995.

Robert Warren, *Living Well*, HarperCollins, 1998.

We are what we do, *Change the World for a Fiver*, Short Books Ltd, 2004

Filmography

Frank Darabont (director), *The Shawshank Redemption*, Castle Rock Entertainment, 1984.

Hugh Hudson (director), *Chariots of Fire*, Twentieth Century Fox, 1981.

Jean-Pierre Jeunet (director), *Amélie*, Momentum, 2001.

Roland Joffe (director), *The Mission*, Warner Brothers, 1986.

E is for discipleship

Running Alpha, Christianity Explored or another Christian basics course and struggling to know what to do next? Looking for small group material that's not mind-bogglingly academic or mind-numbingly shallow? Help is at hand.

The 'Emmaus – the Way of Faith' discipleship material offers a library of stand-alone modules that are designed to help Christians develop and grow. Each module is split into four or five sessions which provide material for Bible study, discussion, group exercises, meditations, practical application and prayers. There's plenty of background material for leaders and a series of downloadable handouts for each member of the study group.

Emmaus encourages a journey of faith that is life-changing, enduring and that has a positive impact on the community of believers, as well as the individual.

 Curious? Call 020 7898 1451 today and request a FREE Introduction to Emmaus Pack, email emmaus@c-of-e.org.uk or visit **www.e-mmaus.org.uk** for full details.

Emmaus – the first word in discipleship